TOBIAS AND THE DRAGON

A Hungarian Folk Tale

Val Biro

Blackie
London

Bedrick/Blackie
New York

Once upon a time there was a poor man called Tobias. He lived in a little cottage with his wife and children. And soon they had so many children that there wasn't enough money to feed them all.

So one fine day Tobias decided to set out to seek his fortune.

'When I come back there will be enough for all of us,' he told his wife as he kissed her goodbye. Then he put a piece of cream cheese in his pocket and went on his way.

Tobias walked and walked until he came to a meadow. And there, right in the middle of the meadow, stood a dragon — a big fierce dragon belching flames! Tobias was terrified but he knew that fear would get him nowhere, so he bravely marched right up to the dragon.

'Now then, you miserable dragon, what are you doing here?' he demanded.

The dragon was rather taken aback. 'What am *I* doing here? This meadow belongs to *me* if you must know!'

'We'll soon see about that,' said Tobias boldly. 'Let's have a contest — and I warn you, I'm terribly strong!'

The dragon was very suspicious, but he agreed.

Tobias picked up a piece of rock and gave it to him. 'See what you can squeeze out of *this!*' he said.

Without a word the dragon grabbed the rock and, huffing and puffing, crumbled it into dust.

'Not bad,' said Tobias, 'but I can do better. I can squeeze cream cheese out of rock!'

He picked up another rock, took the cream
cheese secretly out of his pocket, pressed
it against the rock and squeezed. The
dragon saw something dripping
from the stone and tasted it.

'It's cream cheese all right,' he said, much impressed.
'Well, if you are *that* strong, let's be friends — come
home and meet my family!' So they walked on side by
side until they reached the dragon-village.

They found the rest of the family at supper in the big
dragon-house. Father dragon gave Tobias a hard stare, but
the dragon said, 'This is my friend. And you must be nice
to him because he is terribly strong and if you make him
cross he will destroy the lot of us!'

So mother dragon asked Tobias to sit down and have
supper. The stew was so delicious that he ate more than
all the dragons put together.

For a whole week the dragons were most polite to their guest — in case he got cross and destroyed them all. Tobias had breakfast in bed every morning, and by the time he got up it was time for lunch. He kept on eating until suppertime, and when he finished supper it was bedtime again. And all the while he did absolutely nothing else.

One day mother dragon had had enough of this. 'I think it's about time you did some work, Tobias. Go and fetch some water from the well.' Tobias knew he could never budge the huge dragon-bucket, but he had an idea.

'If I carry the bucket, I won't be able to see the road,' he said to his dragon-friend. 'Why don't you show me the way?' And the silly dragon went with Tobias, carrying the bucket himself.

As soon as they arrived, Tobias began to dig a trench right round the well.

'What are you doing?' enquired the dragon.

'I am taking the well home,' replied Tobias, 'to save us having to fetch water every day!'

The dragon cried in dismay, 'You can't do that! Seven dragon-villages use this well and if you take it away there will be war!'

Tobias stopped digging and said, 'Well, in that case you can fetch the water yourself!' So the dragon filled the bucket, put it on his shoulder with Tobias on top of it, and they went home.

Next day mother dragon sent them to fetch wood from the forest. The dragon soon got to work, tearing up trees by the roots, as was his custom. Tobias was alarmed because he could hardly have broken a twig by himself, but he had an idea.

He tied a rope right round the forest and said, 'I'll take the whole forest home to save us from having to fetch wood every day!'

'You can't do that!' cried the dragon in dismay. 'Seven dragon-villages use this forest and if you take it away there will be war!'

'Well, in that case you can fetch the wood yourself!' said Tobias. So the dragon tore up more trees, put them on his shoulder with Tobias on top of them, and they went home.

Mother dragon was angry to see this. 'What kind of a dragon are you?' she said to her son. 'That Tobias is making a fool of you. You must get rid of him, or else you can leave yourself right now!' The dragon scratched his head — what was he to do? He thought very hard until he had an idea.

'I challenge you to a fight,' he said to Tobias. 'If you win you can have a barrel of gold. But if you lose, you must go home!'

Now it was Tobias who scratched his head — what was he to do? He thought hard until *he* had an idea. 'Very well, but on one condition. You can choose the weapons, but I'll choose the place.'

'Right!' said the dragon fiercely. 'We'll fight with sticks!' And he tore up a great tree-trunk for a stick, and Tobias picked up an axe-handle.

'Come on, dragon, we'll fight in the pigsty!' he said.

But in the tiny sty the dragon could hardly move, let alone fight. So Tobias thrashed him with the axe-handle until the dragon cried for mercy, and gasped, 'You win — take the barrel of gold!'

Then the dragon, to try and get his own back, suggested a sneezing competition. They went into the dragon-house, and the dragon sneezed with such a roar that Tobias nearly stuck to the ceiling. When he recovered, however, he began to stuff bits of rag into the cracks of the wall.

'Why are you stuffing the cracks?' asked the dragon.

'So that they won't let out my sneeze,' said Tobias. 'This way I'll be sure that when I *do* sneeze, the house explodes!' he said.

The dragon fell on his knees and begged Tobias to spare their poor house. 'Take another barrel of gold instead,' he cried.

Then the dragon suggested a shouting competition. 'Very well,' said Tobias, 'but go to the blacksmith first and have your head hooped in iron. Otherwise it will crack apart when I *do* shout!' That was enough for the dragon and he quickly measured out a third barrel of gold. He knew when he was beaten.

Now that he had so much gold, Tobias decided to go home. So he tied his three barrels on the dragon's back, sat himself on top and said, 'Gee-up!' The dragon trotted on meekly, and on the way people laughed to see such a fierce dragon trotting so much like a tame horse. But at last they reached Tobias' house. The dragon was much relieved to have got rid of his dangerous friend at last, said goodbye and happily set off home.

On his way he met a fox. 'What kind of a dragon are you?' sneered the fox. 'That Tobias is a well-known cheat and he's made a right fool of you. Come back with me and for a cock and nine chickens I will get back your gold!'

The dragon felt like a fool right enough and it made him angry. He would get his gold back and destroy Tobias into the bargain! So he marched back with the fox, belching flames.

Tobias saw them coming. Oh dear! If he didn't think of something very quickly *now*, he'd certainly be destroyed and no mistake! Just in the nick of time, sure enough, he *did* have an idea. He scowled angrily and shouted at the fox, 'What's this? Didn't you promise to get me *nine* dragonskins you rascal? Do you mean to fob me off with this *one* miserable dragon?'

The dragon was so alarmed to
hear this that in his fright he
trampled over the fox, took
to his heels and didn't stop
running until he got home.

As for Tobias, he built a fine house with all his gold, big enough for all his family. And the dragons are still as frightened of him as if he had a dragon for breakfast every day.